Time in a

COPY NO. 2

Green Country

Time in a Green Country

Elizabeth Philips

COTEAU BOOKS

Edited by Anne Szumigalski.

Cover photograph by Courtney Milne. Detail of original photograph.

Book design by Joyce Sotski.

Typeset by Lines and Letters.

Printed and bound in Canada by Hignell Printing Limited.

Grateful acknowledgement is made to the following for permission to reprint previously published material:
Collins Publishers for lines on pp. 47 and 54 from *Green Inheritance*, by Anthony Huxley © 1984. Used by permission.
Grossman Publishers for lines on p. 23 from *Hard Labor*, by Cesare Pavese © 1976. Used by permission.
McClelland and Stewart Ltd. for lines on p.1 from *Afterworlds*, by Gwendolyn MacEwen © 1987. Used by permission.
NC Press Ltd, for lines on p. 57 from *Weeds in Canada*, by Clarence Frankton and Gerald A. Mulligan © 1987. Used by permission.

The publisher gratefully acknowledges the financial assistance of the Saskatchewan Arts Board, the Canada Council and the Department of Communications.

Canadian Cataloguing in Publication Data

Philips, Elizabeth
   Time in a green country

   Poems.
   ISBN 1-55050-005-8

I. Title.

PS8581.H44T5 1990   C811'.54   C90-097025-1
PR9199.3.P44T5 1990

C O T E A U   B O O K S
Suite 401–2206 Dewdney Avenue
Regina, Saskatchewan
Canada S4R 1H3   5|6|92

This book is for D.

Contents

PART III   TALES FROM THE GREEN REVOLUTION

1

Open Water

"Because you are beautiful I will have to tell you
a number of my secrets."

Gwendolyn MacEwen, *Afterworlds*

THE ORCHID FANCIER, NORWICH, 1905

We walked along the rows of orchids
and the orchid grower recited their names:
Phalaenopsis, Sobralia, Paphiopedilum, Cymbidium,
Vanda, Brassavola.

I had him write them down
so I could learn to say them. The flower
he cut for me, *Paphiopedilum niveum*, the lady's-
slipper

I held close to my bodice
where it was vibrantly white against the dark green
cloth, the greenhouse progeny of an asiatic flower.

I had been sent by my father to visit this stooped
old man, a crusty fellow with long tapered fingers
as delicate and tremulous as a young plant.

He named for me the parts of the flower:
sepal, petal, column, stigma, anther.
I looked closely
at the bloom, the white flesh
and I could have cried over it, this slight
elegant creature, some kind of offering
I didn't understand.

"The flower is male and female both," he said.
"These are blossoms from before the Fall,
sent to us from Paradise."

HISTORY I

When his daughter-in-law died, Grandfather Peake carried his infant child, Florence Peake, ten days old, to Piccadilly Station, London. He gave her to one of the passengers, with instructions to leave the baby with his sister, Jane Smith, of Moulton, Norfolk.

This is how Florrie came to live with her Aunt Jane, whom she called Mother.

FLORENCE PEAKE AT LODDEN, 1918

I

Carefully posed by the photographer, she sits decorously in a canvas-back chair, surrounded by the sepia foliage of a garden where she is usually more at ease. The chair is striped and her long white dress is covered in small flowers. The flowers are blue and the chair is two shades of green divided by thin strips of yellow. Sturdy beet leaves grow just behind where she sits, purple roots swelling under the earth. The ground is dry, though where her shoes have cut into the soil a black loam is visible, moist from recent rain. The photographer murmurs a warning, and she tenses, holds herself in place.

II

In the letter, my mother writes, "We have had miserable weather for a month now. Your father has had to put the horses in the barn each night." She goes on to say she has had evening grosbeaks at the birdfeeder, that the unrelenting cold weather has kept her indoors, that their taxes have gone up again.

A magpie has lighted in the spruce opposite my kitchen window. It hops from bough to bough, long tail waving in the air like a loose rudder. The tail, I know, has a blue-black sheen which I could see if the sun was shining this morning, or if the tree was closer.

III

After the photograph has been taken, she rises and turns to the garden. Her eyes find a few weeds she has missed, and she stoops to gather some beans for the evening meal. The air smells heavily of greenery steaming in the mid-day sun. Perhaps she thinks of Maggie in *The Mill on the Floss*, or of some fragment from Shelley, perhaps, "The purple flowers are mine, which die while they glow." The earth is warm and moist, and she pushes her fingers deeper into it than necessary. She squats there a minute, forgets her poise and the presence of the camera, the new scientific eye she will never quite grow accustomed to.

IV

The wind has come up and the massive branches violently shudder. The magpie perches close to the trunk, teetering drunkenly as the thickly driven snow sifts through the dark green needles. The picture is a good one, the details sharp. I notice her shiny shoes, open at the top, inappropriate really for the garden, and as in most of her pictures, her mouth is a little strained, she has been unable to smile.

I recall that the English magpie is much the same as this fellow, a scolding nest-robber with a muted sheen, an uncommon brilliance when caught out by the sun, but plain black and white at any distance.

V

She turns again and looks at the photographer. He has packed up his equipment and stands watching her. A youngish man with a thin mustache and a grave professional air. He would have liked to photograph her as she is now, one hand smoothing her hair, a handful of yellow beans held loosely in the other. She is about to offer him a cup of tea. He hasn't the time, he's an apprentice with another appointment in half an hour. She steps toward him, smiling, a smudge of earth on her cheek. She is hoping he will refuse. She wants to change into her gingham, have her tea in the kitchen while she scrubs the potatoes, tops and tails the beans. Then she can sit at the white deal table, staring out at nothing; being alone.

VI

It's snowing harder now, almost obscuring the tree and the back fence, and the magpie has flown away, though I didn't see it go. I put aside the letter, lean the photo up against the teapot. She sits in her garden, in an elegant summer dress that flows to the ground. Past her, outside, the city is draped in a white wind. I like this bad weather. I will wait it out, enclosed here. The red wood of the chairs and table, the blue blossoms of the african violet, in this pool of colour, I sit with my grandmother, "Florence Peake at Lodden, 1918." I look at this beautiful woman, my ancestor, and I look away, almost remembering, almost knowing her.

GOING ALONE

She is at ease, travelling
a sea of boundless days
through the streets of foreign cities.

For the first time she is truly
elsewhere. Her entire language
borne inside her, untranslatable.

Suspended for hours, going by train
there's nothing to be done
about anything.

She has become a country.
In the profound and private
absolution of exile, she sleeps

in rooms full of women,
some of them beautiful, she is measuring
within her borders the truth of distance.

HISTORY II

It has been said
she went deaf to avoid the cutting edge of his humour.

It has been said
that she said herself
she would not have married him had she known
he drank so much.

And there is more I have promised not to put
in any poem.

And I remember how
at the end of every visit he gestured for me
to kiss his bald head. I brushed my lips across
the warm pink skin. His smooth round head
smelled of Old Spice and pipe tobacco. I liked that good-bye
kiss.

THE GIFT OF A MOTH ORCHID
SPRING, 1919

As I sit at my desk preparing my first lecture
in the dark hours of the morning,
the orchid is a strong, solid white
with a splash of red and yellow on its ornate lip.
A definite presence, distinct, intact.

And then as the light comes, and the room brightens,
the flower pales, grows translucent, hesitant,
hovering over the small glass vase.
Throughout the morning, while I teach Latin,
the sun creeps across the rows of girls

and the bloom increases in radiance, wavering,
about to take flight, to carry the light on its wings
and out the open window, where the scent of lilac
hangs like a mauve curtain.

At noon, when I close my book and dismiss the students,
I see the moth has finally caught the sun
and a tip of flame breathes on its lip,
while the sepals are only a faint green stain
as the blossom strains to rise out of itself.

THE HOUSE OF MY ENGLISH GRANDMOTHER

I

There is no rest from change.
As a child not knowing the names of plants
or even the colours of their blossoms
I stood at the threshold of the sun room
and drank in the light streaming
from petals and fronds. There's no rest
from the changes of memory.

II

Memory begins with light, with windows.
Rainbows on the carpet where I played
at jacks and pick-up-sticks
while everyone but the kitchen help
was at my other grandmother's funeral.
Someone came and gave me a chocolate.
Excused from mourning I was allowed
to look away from death, to the bevelled
glass. I was happy there
with rainbows on my hands.

III

The grass is littered with leaves and acorns
from the great old oaks. Autumn
and its pale leaning sun, another season
passing. Here I am carefully silent,
and when I move, I move with care and just contained
laughter, through the strict districts
of my grandfather's failing tyranny.
Patiently I raise myself up
and out of childhood, beneath the great
old oaks in the yard.

IV

When older I steal from room
to room, looking for something.
I find letters and telegrams.
Letters from the war, messages of loss
from that other world, where such things
happened. Dark slanting closets, cigar boxes,
crowded desk drawers, all of these speak
with the faint voices of ancestors.
I lose myself in the untended places,
take deep full draughts of this illicit gift,
the freedom of the house.

HISTORY III

Cousins Gilbert and Winnie, originally of Long Stratton, went with Sidney to meet his fiancee, Florrie, at the train station in Calgary. The next day, August 13, 1920, they were married. Florrie had a lovely silk dress in her suitcase, but it was badly crushed, and so she was married in the plain brown suit she had travelled in. Gilbert and Winnie were witnesses. Florrie was 32 and Sidney was 30.

ITALY

I Venice

I look at their faces, rosy from clowning
through the streets, my two new friends, lovely
and open, telling me the names of their sisters
and brothers, taking me with them
out into a night as black as the water.

We sail from island to island
in the back of a vaporetto, singing Christmas carols
over the drone of the engine. "Joy to the World,"
"O Tannenbaum," "We Three Kings," "As Shepherds Watched
Their Flocks By Night." I ache a little

not wanting to part from them,
my two young sweethearts, one on either side of me
as the boat rocks from port to port.
I want to have them always before me

dancing along the alleys, following the signs
to San Marco, foolish tourists, the lifeblood
of a sinking city. I watch their fine clear faces
and am precariously happy, as we sit down to picnic
in a park full of stray cats. We drink white wine,
eat *bel paese*, olive bread, tart yoghurt.
Soon my friends will be gone

on their way back to America, while I am still
caught in the heart of my travels.
On our last evening we sit on our hard beds,
drinking to our luck, our felicity, meeting like this
in the blue-green fog. We are each a little in love

with one another, and Venice, and living on the water.
I watch their faces, listen to their drawl, the drawn-out
syllables. Laughing, we hide the liquor from the sisters,
spilling *Cinzano*, a long dark red pool,
across the cold convent floor.

II Florence

I am resting on the lawn of the *Palazzo dei Congressi*,
waiting for the movies to start in the plush new theatre.
This morning I spent hours in the streets, tramping
in worn-out sneakers, searching shop windows for new boots,
learning the city. An outsider, starkly visible, I tried
to hide amongst the holiday shoppers. Now I am tired out.
I lie in the thick rough grass, eating mandarins and bitter-
sweet chocolate, a stray cat at my feet.

The cat is ginger and white, with one runny eye.
I give it a piece of chocolate, which it eats in quick
delicate bites. A young couple comes to sit nearby,
laughing and talking, singing the Italian cadence.
I close my eyes and in their voices hear the centuries
speaking, ghost upon ghost, layer on layer of event,
the air thick with precedent. I reach to stroke the cat,
but it jumps nervously away.

I gather up my things, brushing at my damp jeans,
and walk stiffly into the theatre, finding a seat
close to the screen. I want to disappear in the dark,
to lose my awkward foreign face. I enjoy the film
because it's in English. Later, undressing in my room,
my shirt smells faintly of good French scent,
leather against skin, the smell of the crowd,
my unknown companions.

III   Rome

In Rome I fall into a routine, eating at the same places each day, brioche and capuccino, pizza and beer, pasta. And walking the same route, Trevi Fountain, *Piazza di Espagna*, *Piazza Navona*, St. Peter's, and back again. I don't speak to anyone except the Italian men who follow me—one poor fellow leaps out of his car along the *Via del Corso*, runs up to me, exclaiming that my face is *molta simpatica*, wanting to buy me coffee. I say no and walk on. He gets back in his car and catches up with me, leaps out again crying *molta simpatica*. I say no and walk on, leaving him leaning against his car, mournful, bereft. I carry on through the city, remembering the night's dreams, lush tropical dreams raining with love, green and sweet as summer. I walk till my legs ache, then stop at a cafe for espresso, sitting outside though it costs three times as much, more at ease on the edge of the crowd. I hardly ever go inside, not until dark. The city smells of damp stone, fog, car exhaust. I can't stop moving, trudging across the grass in the *Villa Borghese* as if it were a field, my face glowing in the close dank air, the weight of the small pack on my back. In Rome, I have arrived, after months of travel, I have reached this plateau—I see myself, striding through the crowds, in love with possibility, riding some kind of pagan ecstasy as if I were born for rapture.

WITH THE AUNTS AT HEMSBY, NORFOLK, 1985

I loved the aunts, their deep voices,
their infirmities, cataract and forgetfulness.
Who does she look like? they wondered.
Sidney, they said and smiled. *She looks like
Sidney* (the mean older brother).
*But don't bother, you are yourself
and your face is your own.*

They pour tea into my cup
again and again. *We swim in the stuff*,
they murmur, pouring out.

Mary got them talking about the war.
*One day we went down to the sea
for our usual walk, and the beach was covered
in oranges. The whole village was out,
gathering mandarins into bags and baskets,
the cargo of a wrecked ship.*

*We stuffed a few into our pockets.
They were good oranges all right,
sweet and firm, a real treat it was.*

Leaving, they kissed me, and their cheeks
were silky and warm, moist as moss roses.
I loved the aunts, their deep schooled voices
and their infirmities, rheumatism
and forgetfulness.

HISTORY IV

I dreamed of my grandmother bathing
in a huge old-fashioned tub
in the open air by the lake.
The tub stood on a wooden dock jutting out
into the harbour. Her body
was large and creamy white, and her nakedness
was an old nakedness, her skin was pinched
and drawn tightly across her bones.
And her long grey hair, fine and silken,
flowed down her shoulders and into the water.
She was beautiful and I feared for her.
The wind blew coldly and the waves
slid against the pier. I wanted
to cover her up, to shield her
from that stretch of open water.

HISTORY V

"My Dear Jane," she wrote,
"Spring came in at 6:07 this evening according
to the paper. We are still living in a white
world. When will this snow go? It will soon
be April." The snow fell in abundance that year,
two and three feet deep it was, the winter of 1974.
She was 87 and it was cold.

"I do miss getting out but everywhere
has been so icy and the snow is so deep,
I feel better and safer at home."
She poured over seed catalogues, dreamed
of spring and the garden her son would work
into a green splendour, of the first salad,
lettuce leaves only, born of water and earth.

"We have a window full of lovely blooms right now,
hyacinths, daffodils and today one pot of tulips."

One evening a TV program on gardening foretold
an infestation of worms for the coming summer.
That night she couldn't sleep. She saw before her
the rose bushes alive with worms, their flowers half-open,
eaten by insatiable white mouths. She was haunted
by lines from Blake, "the invisible worm
that flies in the night . . . has found out thy bed
of crimson joy, and his dark secret love
does thy life destroy."

On the back of the letter she has absently written,
"Spirit of the Living God fall afresh on me."

Finally in June spring arrived, and the huge
accumulation of snow flooded the yard.
Tender green shoots sprouted in the flower boxes.
But there was little rain all summer,
and by August drought had set in,
the earth cracked and there were no worms.

KATHERINE MANSFIELD

". . . so that I may be
(and here I have stopped and waited and waited
and it's no good—there's only one phrase
that will do) a child of the sun."

She spoke with me on a train on the French Riviera.
She sat by the window, coughed between sentences,
turning to stare at the Mediterranean.
Of course I'd like to tell you

what she said, but I don't know how to say it.
She was more radiant even than that sea,
and her understanding
reached beyond me.
She had come to some conclusions.

All I can tell you is
she spoke about her suffering
as if it had become a kind of love.

CLOCKWORK I

Flies hover around her face, they land in her hair,
but she doesn't brush them away.
Her feet hurt because they are cold.
They are out of her reach
and the blanket over her knees doesn't cover them,
not much she can do about it.
The sun is distant, but it colours her face,
and her skin catches the scent of fallen leaves.

The yard, the little she can see of it,
looks flat as a postcard. The sweetpeas
at the bottom of the garden are a smudge of pink
and red. She hears nothing but intimate sounds,
her breath like the flap of a sail
filling and emptying, the creak of her neck
when she turns her head.

Inside the dark draughty house nothing changes.
The sun leaks thinly in the windows, she can't
get her hands on it. And throughout the house
she encounters the vigilance of clocks.
The grandfather clock in the downstairs hall
is stopped, hands folded together on twelve.
The pendulum has been still for over ten years,
yet she finds herself believing it.

On her bedside table a round army-green alarm clock
clacks. She can't hear it, but each night
when she winds it, she can feel the mechanism
knocking away inside. Awake in the dark, cloaked
in a painful sleeplessness, she watches the luminous hands
slowly circle, winding down toward dawn.

The other face, keeper of daylight hours,
the clock on the mantelpiece, presides over the livingroom,
its wooden wings spread like the all-embracing
arms of an icon, like the statues of Mary
of Jesus blessing the worshipful.
She studies its huge bland face, but to no avail,
she loses track. She cannot make the minutes count.

Preferring to be out, as she is this morning,
she hums a little, settled stiffly in her chair.
A hymn marches through her head, the tune pulled
from memory. She goes over the verses several times,
singing to herself, that repeating rhythm
bears her forward. "Faith of our Fathers,
living still," she recites, recalling the evening
when as a child of eleven she had sung the same lines,
alone, wandering home from church.

She had stood under an apple tree and had heard
a nightjar call. She'd paused, then had sung out
a refrain, and the bird had whistled, as if replying.
"We shall be true to thee till death"
she sings now, addressing that distant shadow
falling across her path. She sings purposefully,
getting the words right, until the morning has passed
and it's time to go in.

TO THE MEMORY OF FLORENCE PEAKE

The house will be sold out of the family.
I walk quickly through the cold rooms, then retreat,
go out into the yard where summer comes at me
full tilt, a mass of yellow lilies.
On the far side of the garden I find
she is survived by the columbine, a perennial
that has thrived despite the hard winters
since her death.

Bending down for a closer look, I see
how the nodding green buds resemble
proud exotic birds. And soon the beaks will crack
and open into slender purple bells.
I lie down in the grass, focus on the tight
unopened flowers, the concealed
luster.

It was in this garden she grew reconciled
to a place where plants are sly and withholding,
lie in false senescence, suspended,
waiting for spring. Here she worked the ground,
her head clamouring with rich and hopelessly
remote detail. I watch her
across an irrevocable distance.

Eventually, I stand and turn to leave, only pausing
for a minute at the gate. Looking back, I can pick out
the rising columbine. I am reluctant
to let the place go. But I have no say in it
and must make do with this last viewing,
at least having seen what remains
of her time in a green country.

II

Safe Home

"Sleeping on the street
shows confidence in the world."

Cesare Pavese, *Hard Labor*

L DREAMS

Her body is slick as a fin, and she skims over the lake like a
blade. She assumes the water with a natural ease,
breathes in the dangers.

She dives under, swims into the weeds, mouth open, leaving no
trace on the surface. Only to re-appear farther out, breaking
the smooth blue-black skin of the lake,

a laugh beating somewhere near her heart.

IN EUROPE NOW MY OTHER SELF IS SLEEPING

The first snow lies along my shoulders
like an embrace, familiar touch, and strange
after autumn's dry fingertips.

I am settling in, home from a long journey
some months. I look up at the huge flakes
rushing at me like stars.

A cool white hand draws across my eyes,
loosing memory.
I have never been anywhere else

but here,
going nowhere through the thickly falling snow.

L SPEAKS OF ORIGINS

She was born by a tremendous lake, in a leonine March,
a blizzard gusting over the ice, the huge thick floes
locking and unlocking, an ever-changing geography.
Later, she would learn the language of ice, of snow,
the slippery joy, the treacherous surface of things.

The records claim she was born in another place, a city
wired together with hydro poles, a place where two rivers
met, a confluence of polluted waters. A mistake, of course—
the scene is unimaginable.

She denies this paper evidence, emphatically.

She was born on the shores of Lake Winnipeg
in the last big storm before spring,
all definition lost in snow raked by a pure wind,
the air viciously cold and bright and virgin.

TRANSLATION

On the riverbank, I'm completely alone,
no one passing.

A fox darts up the bank,
blond arrow with certain direction
it pauses to look at me, then disappears.

This is not what I expected—
a fox retreating like a torn flag,
the last wild thing.

There must be other creatures in the undergrowth,
mole-like, subversive, dreaming dreams
of the entirely natural.

A pale uncertainty, the vision of the fox
remains. I feel the loss of something.
Turn and walk back up into the city.

CONSIDER THE SEA

Last night the last thing you let fall
was your watch.
We entered the evening

and how my mouth
found the secret place
divining there a measure of the sea

while time lay face down
on the floor
lost in the folds of your blouse.

*

Now, cut adrift, lonely in the certainty of loss
I imagine for comfort
                    the sea, its entirety:

sea-bed, mollusk, anemone, coral, shark.
The obscure worlds turning there.
I imagine the red welt of sky at dawn,
how the water weaves and shines.

I lie very still
like a beached star, a creature
gathering in radiance, listening
for the monumental breathing of the sea.

THE FIRST AND ONLY LESSON IS BREATHING

I get no pay for the work I do.
A woman who makes love to women, I teach
appreciation of the female.
The first and only lesson is breathing
deeply our wild smell: stamen and pistil
in hot sun; rich forest floor; darkness.

Their priests detest and fear me—the women
miss church on my account.
Lying late in my bed they sing and sweat,
anointing my face with their juices.
They are easily instructed—they eat me up,
my body so like their own.

I work for the pleasure of their pleasure.
Like sleepwalkers in daylight, they come to me,
one at a time, to learn what they know.
                    And when they come,
the sins of the fathers are displaced
by the spirit returning. And their minds clear,
like the sky arching over us
in the solemn quiet of Sunday morning.

L STAYS HOME AND WATCHES THE ORCHIDS GROW

L is obsessed with plant culture. She spends hours reading through her copy of *Success With Houseplants*, studying each entry thoroughly. She's pleased to discover she can feed the boston fern with the orchid fertilizer. Getting up to do this immediately, she remembers that she really ought to be working, sticking labels on a huge stack of envelopes. This is the kind of work she gets, odd jobs she can do at home, so she can tend to the plants. L doesn't go out much. Not for months now, not since she went away for a few days to visit friends, and when she came back she found *Phalaenopis amabilis* had dropped its buds. First thing in the morning, still dreamy, she feels the thick green leaves of each orchid, lifts their pots, judges by weight whether they need water. Their long green flower spikes, knotted with buds, emerge so slowly, it takes months. She just can't afford to lose the promise of flowers. She sits by the plants at night, reading *Orchids and Serendipity*. Maybe she should try cattleyas, the sweetly scented corsage orchid, she decides, feeling a thrill of anticipation, or even *Laeliocattleyas*, a hardy hybrid available in an exotic choice of colours.

L ON THE PROWL

Downtown one drizzly afternoon L falls in behind a stranger, a woman in a shiny red raincoat. The woman is dark and thin, with pale olive skin stretched over sharp high cheekbones. She is sleek, like a small animal. L trails after her in the rain, trying to be inconspicuous, though there isn't much of a crowd to hide in; she has gone out without her umbrella and her cotton sweater is soon quite damp. The red raincoat steps into a small jewelry shop. L stands in front of the window pretending to admire the rows of gaudy engagement rings. Covertly, she stares at the woman, pleased by her deft movements, by her long tapered fingers holding the hair out of her eyes as she bends over a display case. The woman tries on a ring, smiles at her glittering hand, revealing small pointed feral teeth. L flinches, surprised. Suddenly, she feels hugely hungry. She pivots on her heel and with a sense of urgency, the rain drumming harder now, runs to catch a bus home.

THE DARK SIDE OF L

L is beseiged by terrible weather.
One day she wakes up heavy
with rain, swollen
with the condensation of sorrow.
Reluctant to rise, she lies under
the stale covers, curled up,
rubbing her cold feet in her hands.
When she hauls herself up,
she stares sullenly at the crowd
of plants in each window,
splashes water on one or two.

This inclemency cannot be foretold.
Though she ought to see it coming,
it takes her by surprise every time,
a black pall descends, seeded
with despair. Her friends know
the symptoms, L's eyes are overcast,
her smile is grey. She complains
of aching joints, lethargy, dislocation.
This goes on for days.

When the end comes she is suddenly
electric, bristling with energy
and dry good humour.

The cloud has burst, the blood has come.

GOOD FRIDAY

Everything flowers,
surely?
she said crossing the street
sloppy with water and melting snow

No, I said, lagging behind,
getting my feet wet.
No, I don't think
so.

L AND *P. LADY RUBY 'YOUTHFUL'*

L faces up to it. The flower spike on her *P. Lady Ruby 'Youthful,'* has to go. The plant is too weak to bear flowers, has only two old leaves and no sign of a new one. She got it cheap from a florist, half the leaves blasted by frost. If she doesn't snip the spike, it may literally flower itself to death. She should do it now, before the buds appear, before curiosity takes hold: she's never seen the Lady in bloom. L turns away to admire the hibiscus. The huge red flowers, open for one day only, greedily gather the morning light. She sterilizes the clipper blades with a flaming match, then clips the spike. Bending over, she brushes against a hibiscus flower and a streak of orange pollen flares across the pocket of her white shirt.

STICK WOMAN

Days when I am all edges, my hands are young,
dumb and grasping they bang and tear
and you wonder where the love is.
Then, saddened, I am all insides, like a thing
just killed, or new born, pink
and tender as a weeping eye.

But this is a secret; you can't tell
from the outside my unfinished places:
a full moving form hides stark black lines
and blank planes, a child's drawing of herself.

L DREAMS AGAIN

Her father's horse is in trouble, a bay gelding,
it gallops across the thin fall ice
while L runs along the shore, her bare feet cutting
through cold wet sand.
                        The ice is so thin
she imagines she can see waves rippling beneath it.

As the horse spins across the diaphanous lake
her father roars its name. At the water's edge, L stumbles,
her face inches from the daintily feathered ice,
a fogged window.

The horse disappears as her father lunges toward it,
plunges his arms into the freezing water,
groping for the mane. She calls to her father then,
shouts for him to come back to shore, but he doesn't hear

and she watches as the horse sinks again and again
bones gone rubbery, eyes gone white.

CLOCKWORK II

My love,
listen here. Not just to the heart,
no,

but to the entire body, loaded as it is
with little clocks, hundreds
of chemical ticks, secretions,
migrations.

The names of their rhythms
sound like this:
ultradian, infradian,
circasemiseptan,
circadian, circavigintan,
circannual, circadiseptan.

The most usual is circadian,
a cycle of between 20 and 28 hours,
or roughly the length of a day.

And it is all rough, biological
clocks are not exact, no,
they are all more or less,
give or take a few hours or days,
a few weeks or months.

Listen. Though all you hear tonight
is the heart, a powerful and inaccurate
measure, I have to say, the heart
is not top clock, no, not nearly.

There is no maestro, no master.
We have wanted a boss rhythm, to keep the body
in tune, to keep our house in order.
But we have to admit it, nothing
is that simple.

The body makes successful noise,
not music exactly, but a workable cacophony,
everything happening at once,
connected, disconnected,
independent, interdependent.

My love, this is what I have wanted to say.
That we are composed of time, and time
is not one thing only, precise,
bang-on, like a wristwatch,
nor is it the wonderfully wound-up
hierachy of clocks.

So I leave you with these few words,
make of them what you will: disorder,
accident, randomness, disarray,
discord, confusion,

pure chance.

SEPTEMBER, 1984

When the wasps began in the fall
there were only a few each morning
in the front window.
They came in through a kitchen cupboard
dropped onto the counter
and flew into the living room.
A week later there were hundreds. I tired
of killing them with a newspaper, and frankly
all that death in the morning made me sad.
A few came upstairs to my bedroom
and at night crawled into
my dreams. When winter finally came
the invasion stopped.

A house full of wasps. It seemed appropriate then.
My love was on the wane and they kept me company.
I was never stung.

III

Tales from
the Green Revolution

"The grass withereth, and the flower thereof falleth away."

I Peter 1:24

FOUR SMALL POEMS FOR THE GRASSES

"A child said *What is the Grass?*
fetching it to me with full hands."
—Walt Whitman, *Leaves of Grass*

I

Grama grass.   Little bluestem.
Ticklegrass.   The wild grasses
grow in preserved areas, along roadsides,
in ditches, on land too rocky
for cultivation,
                    anywhere
marginal.

June grass.   Bluejoint.   Holy grass.

Too many to name.   The grasses surrender
their seed to the air, pollinate
in the hot dry rushes of wind.

Big bluestem.   Canary reed.   Poverty grass.

II

The grasses are the family
Gramineae.

Their narrow leaves have parallel veins,
the stems are round and hollow, and the flowers
are the most neglected of blooms,
not listed
in *Wildflowers Across the Prairies*.

The intimate ground is rife with slight
signs. More precise than the words

sheath, blade, auricle, umbel. The inflorescence,

the arrangement of minute flowers on the stem,
is crucial in the telling
of one grass from another, a subtle
articulation, beyond the sounding out of syllables.

III

A bare stretch of black prairie is not barren—
the roots of bunch grass are so dense, nothing can grow there,
not even grass.

Grass grows from the base, when you slice off the tops,
grass will come back, bloom
more vigorously than ever.

Most of grass thrives in secret,
expands underground. One rye plant
has over three hundred miles of roots.

I salt away such details.
I believe in the end they may be necessary,
they may be useful.

IV

Blue-eyed grass is not a grass,
but an iris.
Black grass is not a grass,
but a rush.
Brown sedge is not a sedge,
but a grass.

How the common names of things mislead,
obscure, misconstrue. The accidents of lore
rcvcal impaticncc, a willingncss
to abuse.

Generous, benevolent, the grass covers full
one-third of the world. Haphazardly named, trampled
into dust, ground into flour

grass is the sun come down
to root in the earth, to burn in the veins of all
the careless indifferent animals.

YOUNG JACK

He stands at the edge of the spruce bluff surrounding the old well built by a Hungarian who worked for his grandfather. His dad intends to fill it in, but never finds the time. Jack fears that old well, fears that his dog will stumble into its open mouth. He heads for the fields, avoiding the bush altogether, whistling for the dog, a young collie. Jack stops in the middle of the field, lies down in the hay and the sky lies over him, deep blue. The dog sniffs his boots, then settles down to lick her paws. Jack tries not to think of the well. Though a beautiful thing it is, built in the first years of the century, built by hands out of rocks only. He has bad dreams about it, but he keeps them to himself. He has nightmares about falling in, about his older brother trapped far down, his bones broken, drowning in its stagnant water. The thing tears a hole in his sleep and he plunges into the depths. He wonders what would happen if he were to look at it, tells himself it's only an old hole with a little brackish water at the bottom. He almost thinks to lower a cup and haul up the harmless salt taste of it. But he shys away from this bold picture of himself. He prefers his nightmares, confining danger to a sleeping vertigo, to the small room in the basement where he dreams, wrapped tightly in the sheets.

BROTHERS AND OUTSIDERS

The grounds of our monastery are bordered by bush,
a cultivated woodland. I follow the wide
careful paths, precisely cut and mowed by my brethren.
I can't get lost here, unable to forget even for a moment
the human. But hot summer nights when I fall asleep

I find my world changed, I'm dumped
into the thick of real wilderness, and it's burning.
The trees crack and fall, the terrified fleeing animals
surge around me, deer and wolf and moose, and I run with them,
the fire a wave of heat soaring at my back.

The skirts of my cassock catch and tear, pull me
down, my legs kicking. I see the others,
the nimble creatures, flying toward escape,
while I collapse, rooted in my terrible body,
ashamed.

All night the smoke billows like a huge black wing
and I struggle for air. Inside I am on fire, my heart,
my lungs. I heave and strain, until at last I reach the river,
lurch headlong into the warmth of it, water the colour
of daylight.

Morning returns me to the slow certain routine
of the brothers, and a few chosen outsiders.
Here, I tell myself, I am safe. This is the only lie
I don't confess. Twenty years within these walls,
and still, when I close my eyes, I run, I burn.

LANGUAGE

there is no discipline like winter
say what we will   our breath
hangs   in this white and level land
we address ourselves with caution

the bitter   the stark
cold   nothing as precise as blue
a cut above other colours
in the morning

small birds call to one another
punctuate the quiet
with fine thin notes   a song of domain
of limits

the land
and what we make on the land
what has been spoken

a map   ancestral soundings

we open our mouths and dreams float out
we say "house" and trees fall

we are one voice in awe of this extreme
pain an edge at least   a particular end
the cold measures the day
we can only go so far

we live here because we can
we follow the exacting line of earth
and sky   that vastness
we people with our careful imaginings

we are hesitant   afraid
to crack such stillness
with our restraint
with our concise and definite being

we choose this place   finally
it is ours for the saying

TALES FROM THE GREEN REVOLUTION

"The use of these new high-yielding Rice and also Wheat varieties ... has given rise to what is called the 'Green Revolution.'" —Anthony Huxley, *Green Inheritance*.

You walk home from work through snow flecked with grey ash, along streets spilling with cars. Stopped at a corner you watch a man beat on the hood of his stalled car with both fists, his face crimson, his figure wreathed in exhaust from passing vehicles. His car blocks the walkway and you step quickly around it. Living here, on the prairie that is no longer prairie, demands exacting acts of the imagination. You believe the city doesn't count, under the asphalt the land waits to renew itself with russian thistle and pigweed and scarlet globe mallow. You have learned that these are the plants that succeed after the ground has been stripped bare by catastrophe.

You wish to remain true to the prairie. Imagining the buildings gone, you see mile upon mile of blue grama and buffalo grass. You know the names of plants, though you couldn't find them in a field. Wood anemone, gum weed, valerian. You even know their uses—to cure headache, to purify the blood, to ease digestion. Crossing the last jammed intersection before the tree-lined streets of your neighbourhood, you work hard to conjure the blue-white fields beyond the city, the silent tracts of bush, where your fancy hears only the language of trees in the wind, maple, trembling aspen, and spruce.

In the evenings your mind lies fallow. You meditate on the snow-light that hangs between dull overcast and the crested white drifts. Awake late into the night, you lie in bed with the window open a crack, and a restful calm leaks in. You can feel the living presence of the land. You imagine the grass beneath the snow, crumpled under the sleeping weight of the city. Soon you too are asleep, the night covers you in a green darkness and you dream the wet smell of spring, pungent as sweat. You rush down to the river where you stand swaying, out of breath, your body hot as blood, your flesh pulsing. You watch the trees bud, and the buds unfold into leaves the size of your hands.

47

NOW AND THEN

So this is it.
A cup of something hot and sweet,
a view from the porch
of trees and electrical wires,
the planes of a roof.
Days and days of this. The mind
deflected from the page, fixed on
what?

Shadows grow out of the dusk.
A maple tree scatters its seeds
on the gravelled back lane.
In the porch an old upholstered armchair,
a place to sit while time passes.
There is a moon, or there isn't.

And it won't change much, ever.
Trees. Houses. The seasons.
There will be love
and there won't be.

L AND DAMNATION

L has friends over for fettucine. She uncorks the wine, passes it around, and they drink several toasts—to friendship, to a beautiful spring day, to L, to Irving Berlin, whose birthday was the day before. Then they sit down and eat. By the time the first bottle has been emptied, they're arguing religion. L waves her glass, spilling a little, and announces she doesn't buy this business of an afterlife. She pops an olive into her mouth. She who grows things has seen how a root-bound plant eats up the soil, when she shakes it out of the pot there's no dirt left, just a ball of roots. Her friends murmur their confusion. "Wait," she says. "And when a plant dies, I bury it in the yard, where it feeds the earth. The soil grows rich on putrefaction." She's inspired now, she takes a deep breath. "Regeneration is the word. A decaying plant fuels new growth. Only its essence remains. Not the soul, nothing so fancy as that. What's left is raw material. Just *stuff.*" She gulps down a mouthful of wine. "And time. The idea of eternity." She waves her hand dismissively. "All nonsense. This orchid," she points at *P. Lady Ruby 'Youthful'* on the windowsill, "has leaves about 8 inches long, 2 inches wide. And it could live 50 to 100 years. Length, width, depth," she counts the dimensions on her fingers, "volume, and longevity. None of it means anything without this," she raps her knuckles on the table, "the physical world." L sighs, stares darkly into her empty glass, stumped for a moment. She looks out the window, then smiles. "Spring," she says, gesturing at the blossoming apple tree, "now that I can believe in. The seasons. An immeasurable event, spring is." She leans, elbows on the table, and cups her face in her hands, distracted. She dabs her serviette at a stain on the tablecloth. Then she gathers herself up, and declares, "Beyond this," she spreads her arms wide, to embrace the room and the twilit yard beyond, "I can't promise you anything." She stands and refills their glasses from the second bottle, a sour Italian white. "Drink up," she urges, beaming, beneficent.

A LITTLE TOWARD DARK

Several times a day the listing man reels by your window. He tilts down the street, rolling his hips to accommodate his slant on the world. He lives opposite, in the huge old rooming house where everyone is a little strange, a little misshapen. He lurches out each morning to tour the downtown. You know, because you've seen him there, listlessly wandering. Knocked askew by loneliness, he does not meet the eyes that pass by, does not speak to anyone. He cannot stop moving. He returns to his room, only to leave again a few minutes later. As the day wears on he leans more and more to one side, until you think he might fall. But he carries on, only stumbling a little toward dark, accidentally dropping his cigarette. And you, watching safely behind glass, know that loss, of smoke in the lungs, fire in the hand.

DANGER

The worst thing is to know
what's coming, to see
the hands of violence reaching
for you, the bruises
start up before the thumbs meet
at the back of your neck,
to lie down and like a stone
beneath a hammer accept, naturally,
the splintering blow.

DRIVING

The sun was everywhere that morning
as I drove along the highway, going fast like we do,
only the limit, but making good time.
The prairie wind was green
and whistled through the open windows.
I was light and trembling, sure of pleasure,
driving into that unthinkable expanse.
I like to drive, I said to my friend, my passenger.
I want to drive the whole way.
And she was glad to entertain, to talk me
through the miles.

Like everyone, we were behind the times,
innocently looked at our watches to see where we were.
The road pulled the car through the curves.
The city fell away behind me
and I relaxed.

Absolved, I wanted to drive the whole way, swept along
by the generous road, embraced by paved shoulders.
But that morning a deer rose out of the ditch,
running. At first all I saw was grace, a pleasing
glimpse of wilderness, but then it was on the road ahead
and there was no stopping. I closed my eyes
and felt for where the car was,
held to the wheel, and knew at once
I hadn't lost control. I looked out
and found us stopped completely.

I pulled myself up and out, my legs almost giving way.
The grill was caved in, smeared with green guts.
The deer was behind us, had fallen in the long grass,
only its white belly showing; one leg
had been sheared off and was lying on the highway.
We sat down on the slow still ground and waited for help,
our backs to the slain animal.
Grasshoppers were sawing in the weeds.

Hours later, we got into a rented car and drove on.
My friend said she thought the deer knew, its death
was in its eyes. But I shied away, couldn't say anything
for certain. As far as I can remember
nothing shone in those eyes but sunlight.
The rest of the way I studied the fields for movement,
for any sign of wildness, my foot hovered over the brake.
I held on to my fear, drove desperately away
from that black stain pouring into the grass,
my heart spilling in me, knocking me down.

TALES FROM THE GREEN REVOLUTION II

"The revolution has become like a pyramid of cards with the high-
yielding crops balanced precariously on top. Remove the
fertilizer, or the irrigation water, and the stack collapses."
—Anthony Huxley, *Green Inheritance.*

I dream the sound of rain, that rhythm on the windows
and streaming green leaves in a steamy May.
But when I wake a yellow wind is blowing in a yellow sky
and nothing falls from above, nothing but dust.
This is not May, or any other month in the calendar.

I fear the coming summer, day after day of wind, the sun
punishing every green attempt. This Spring is not
the place I expected. The trees slowly force their leaves,
the thick dry air parches my lips, draws a web
of white lines on my hands.

Driving along the highway the dust sifts across the windshield.
I can taste the grit, it crunches between my teeth.
Tumbleweeds roll across the road like spiked wheels.
Like an omen, they flee across the evenly-tilled fields
prepared for rain and seed and herbicides.

I can no longer sustain the romance, this fanciful idea of
prairie. The wind has lifted half the province into the air
and the dust chokes me. I wonder how it is possible to live
in this new world, in the land of the green revolution.
Here the dust is natural, a necessary side effect

of high-tech farms, where every bush and slough
is ploughed under, miles of land left exposed.
I don't know what to call a country where the earth
is a pestilence obscuring the sun. Turning onto a gravel road
the wind gusts against the body of the car

and I tighten my grip on the wheel. The wind carries the truth
home to the city—the soil is a poor commodity this year,
stocks are down, and the market will register certain losses.
Unable to see more than a few feet, I pull over, turn off the car.
Caught in a warm dirty squall, I cover my face with my sleeve.

Stranded by the roadside, I can't escape the country
I have admired and praised, exalting the generous reach
of horizon. I've imagined myself, a westerner, walking the clean
lines of prairie, fingers brushing the flowers of big bluestem,
but all along I was here, eyes closed against the corrupted sky.

JACK GETS A LITTLE SLEEP

Jack sits on a rise in the spruce bluff back of the house.
Two in the morning, and the autumnal darkness, he imagines
is the colour inside his temples, blood-red.

Hard to sleep during harvest, he likes too much the tyranny
of work. By this time each fall he's watching the fields
around the clock. And all the years behind him seem

like another man's happiness. Here on the damp ground,
Jack is nothing, another tired animal sheltering
beneath the creaking ancient conifers.

Jack sleeps in the bloody-black night, his head throbbing
in his hands. He doesn't dream. He goes deep
for what he needs—release, purification,
rest.

When the sky begins to grow light, he starts awake.
He's cramped and stiff, but restored. He's himself again,
old Jack, the last of his family on the land, in love again

with the work, the brutal rhythm of it.
Walking back to the house he's sees the granaries just beginning
to shine in the distance. One of them holds wheat

that is over ten years old. He frowns, says to himself
he's going to move that wheat before he dies.

THE IDEA OF THE WEED

"A weed is a plant that grows where man does not want it to grow, in grainfields, row crops, pastures, hayfields, lawns, and other disturbed areas." —Clarence Frankton and Gerald A. Mulligan, *Weeds in Canada*

Russian thistle, green foxtail, wild oats, goldenrod. I wish to praise the weed, its profligate, infuriating vigour. I cheer its huge excesses, for it endures in swamp, among rocks, in sand, on northern slopes, through dry spells and flood. I admire how the weed persists, wildly successful, how it undermines the big machines, herbicides, the lie of dominion. The weed lives on the real prairie, thrives on drought or rain, whatever offers. It throws off grasshoppers, acid rain, the blistering sun, dust, surging up under our very wheels. I want to praise how the weed anchors topsoil in a windstorm; how it feeds grazing animals when no other forage remains. I congratulate the purple flowers of the common thistle, the yellow of wild mustard. On empty lots, in the back alleys of the city, between downtown warehouses, I defer to the ever-hopeful, stubborn, unkillable weed, for it aspires to nothing but rising again and again.

POEM FROM THE *I CHING*

Hoarfrost is underfoot. Not the season
to begin learning the grasses,
how to know them. No time to search out
at the edge of the city, little bluestem,
the almost invisible flowers.
You know the grass, though you can't translate
palea, lemma, glume, the telltale parts
of the flower, into witch grass, purple-top,
wild rye. You have tasted grass. Rice
and wheat and sugar-cane and corn.

The grass at your feet this morning
is Bermuda. The lawn is fading, the last
green blades tipped with white, first sharp
exhalation, winter rising out of the ground
like cold steam, like it always does.
The grass crunches under your boots. Snow
is not far off. You bend down,
tear clumps of withered marigold
out of the hardening ground.

You consider the roots of the grasses
underlying everything.
Their devotion to the earth
is perfect. Mile upon mile of bristling root
flourishes underground. Soon you will retreat
into the house, where you must wait out
the dark months. You know the grass,
though you can't name by sight the many
native and alien incarnations.

The gathering gloom presses the day
into one bright corner. You crouch
on the dying lawn, fearful of all you can't
give a name to. You vow to continue
your devotions, studying the ways of Gramineae.
Like the grass you will persevere, quietly
under the inevitable weight of ice
and cold. You want to believe
that in the nature of the earth lies the light.

ACKNOWLEDGEMENTS

The author would like to thank the Canada Council Explorations Program, the Saskatchewan Arts Board, the Saskatchewan Writers Guild, and the Saskatchewan Writers/Artists Colonies.

She is grateful for the wisdom and counsel of Susan Andrews, David Carpenter, Lorna Crozier, Paulette Jiles, Patrick Lane, Doris Larson, Anne Szumigalski, and Caroline Heath. And for the support and encouragement of the Philips family, all the incomparable canines, and of course, Pips.

Some of these poems have appeared in *More Garden Varieties*, an anthology of winners of the League of Canadian Poets contest for 1989, *Prairie Fire*, *The Farmshow Catalogue*, *event*, *The Malahat Review*, and *Arc*.

BIOGRAPHY

Elizabeth Philips has had poems published in numerous journals including *Event*, *Fiddlehead*, *The Antigonish Review*, *Freelance*, *The Dinosaur Review*, *Canadian Woman Studies*, *Prairie Fire*, *The Malahat Review* and *Western Living*. Her poetry has also appeared in the anthologies, *Branchlines*, *More Garden Varieties* and Coteau Books's *Heading Out* (1986). A chapbook of poetry, *Breaking Through Ice* was published by Turnstone in 1982.

Originally from Gimli, Manitoba, Elizabeth has lived in Saskatoon since 1980. She graduated from the University of Saskatchewan in 1985 with a B.A. in English. She is a member of the Saskatchewan Writer's Guild, the *NeWest Review* Collective and the Saskatchewan Orchid Society. Elizabeth currently works as a freelance editor and writer.

POETRY FROM COTEAU BOOKS

A selection of poetry titles from Coteau Books is listed below. You may purchase or order any of these titles from your favorite bookstore. For a complete catalogue of our books—fiction, poetry, drama, criticism, non-fiction and children's literature—please write to 401-2206 Dewdney Avenue, Regina, Saskatchewan S4R 1H3.

The Blue Pools of Paradise by Mick Burrs. A poignant collection of wide-ranging poetry. $6.00(pbk), 1983.

Blue Windows by Catherine M. Buckway. New and collected poems with lyric elegance from a prolific writer. $8.00(pbk), 1988.

Changes of State by Gary Geddes. Powerful, arresting poetry by an internationally acclaimed poet. $7.00(pbk), $15.00(cl), 1986.

Earth Dreams by Jerry Rush. Startling images and tightly controlled lyrics reveal new perspectives. $5.00(pbk), 1982.

Going Places by Don Kerr. Poetry that explores the delights of family motoring on the prairie. $6.00(pbk), 1983.

Gringo: Poems and Journals from Latin America by Dennis Gruending. Accessible, powerful writing chronicling Gruending's experiences in Latin America. $6.00(pbk), 1983.

Heading Out: The New Saskatchewan Poets edited by Don Kerr and Anne Szumigalski. A sparkling collection of work by Saskatchewan's newer poets. $9.95(pbk), 1986.

Hold the Rain in Your Hands: Poems News & Selected by Glen Sorestad. Clear, accessible poetry—the best from five earlier collections plus 29 new poems. $8.95(pbk), $15.95(cl), 1985.

Odpoems & by E.F. Dyck. Dyck's first collection of poems, featuring the strange adventures of Od. $4.00(pbk), 1978.

Perishable Light by Dennis Cooley. New poems from an accomplished poet and scholar. $8.00(pbk), $16.00(cl), 1988.

The Secret Life of Railroaders by Jim McLean. The funniest poems ever to roll down the main line. $5.00(pbk) 1982.

Street of Dreams by Gary Hyland. Hyland's themes are found within his own community and are treated with charm and grace. $7.00(pbk), 1984.

A Sudden Radiance: Saskatchewan Poetry by Lorna Crozier and Gary Hyland. This first release in the Carlyle King Anthology Series is a comprehensive collection of work by established poets. $14.95(pbk), $21.95(cl), 1987.

Territories by Elizabeth Allen. A second collection from Allen. Her terrain is the Saskatchewan rural landscape given distinctive treatment. $6.00(pbk) 1984.